LOW VOICE

The Singer's CHRISTIAN HITS

CONTENTS

Page	Song Title	Originally Recorded By	Vocal Demo Track	Accompaniment Track
2	Can't Live a Day	*Avalon*	1	11
8	God Is in Control	*Twila Paris*	2	12
16	The Great Divide	*Point of Grace*	3	13
21	Healing Hands	*Jonathan Pierce*	4	14
27	Heaven in the Real World	*Steven Curtis Chapman*	5	15
34	I Could Sing of Your Love Forever	*SonicFlood*	6	16
41	I Pledge Allegiance to the Lamb	*Ray Boltz*	7	17
46	Let Us Pray	*Steven Curtis Chapman*	8	18
53	A Place Called Grace	*Phillips, Craig & Dean*	9	19
58	We Can Make a Difference	*Jaci Velasquez*	10	20

The recordings in this collection were produced by and licensed from Daywind Soundtracks and are available separately as performance tracks from a music retailer.

ISBN 0-634-04977-1

7777 W. BLUEMOUND RD. P.O. BOX 13819 MILWAUKEE, WI 53213

For all works contained herein:
Unauthorized copying, arranging, adapting, recording or public performance is an infringement of copyright.
Infringers are liable under the law.

Visit Hal Leonard Online at
www.halleonard.com

Can't Live a Day

Words and Music by CONNIE HARRINGTON, JOE BECK and TY LACY

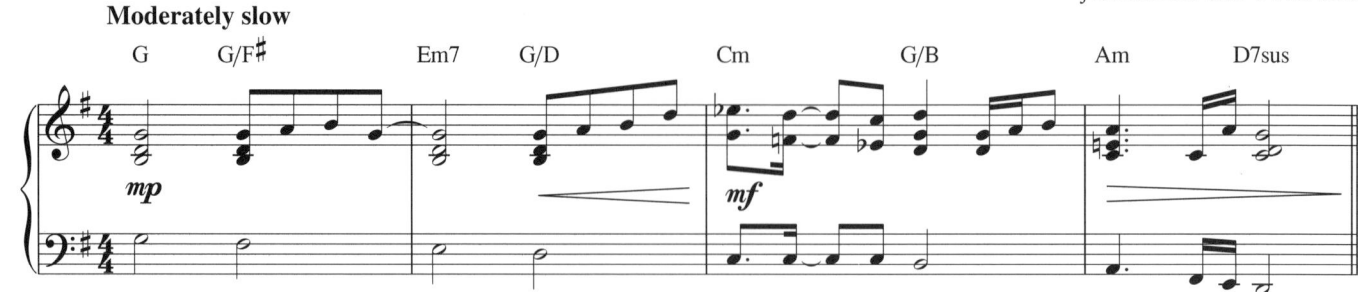

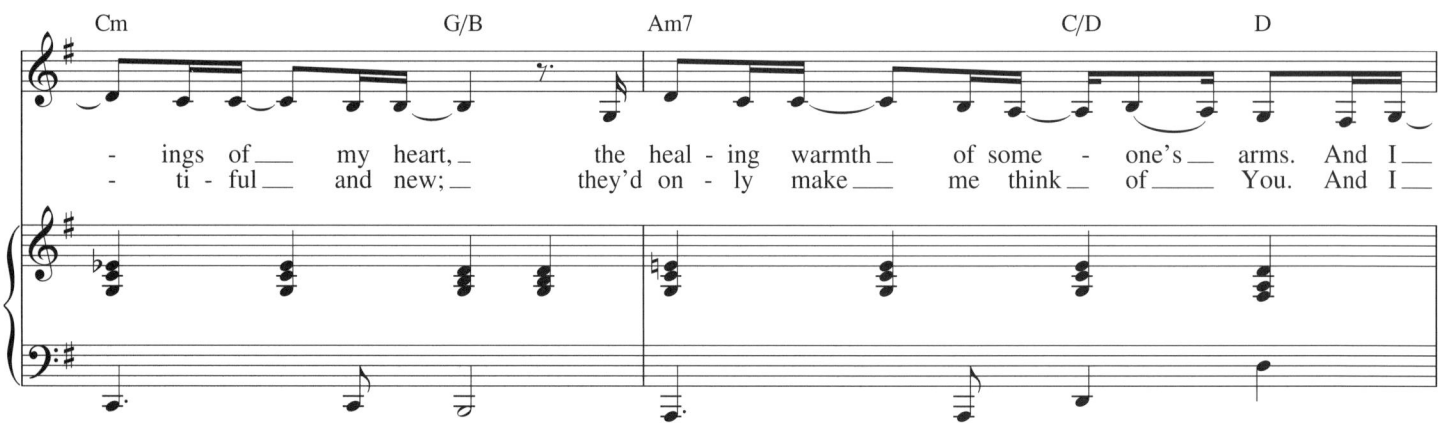
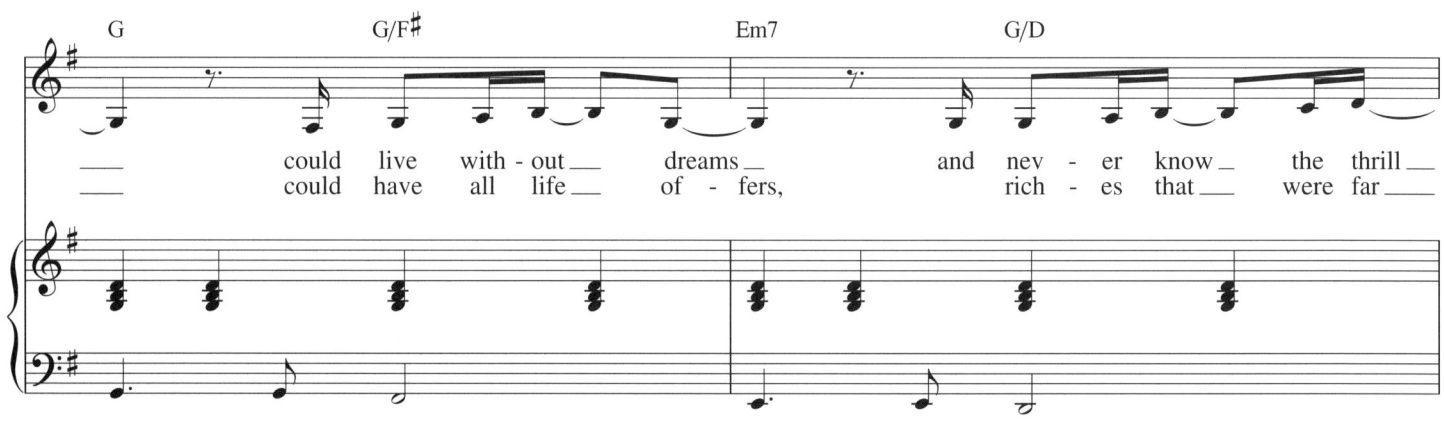

Copyright © 1999 by BMG Songs, Inc., Ariose Music and Bridge Building Music (a div. of Brentwood-Benson Music Publishing, Inc.)
All Rights for Ariose Music Administered by EMI Christian Music Publishing
International Copyright Secured   All Rights Reserved

Lord, there's no night and there's no morning without Your loving arms to hold me. You're the heartbeat of all I do; I can't live a day without You.

God Is in Control

Words and Music by
TWILA PARIS

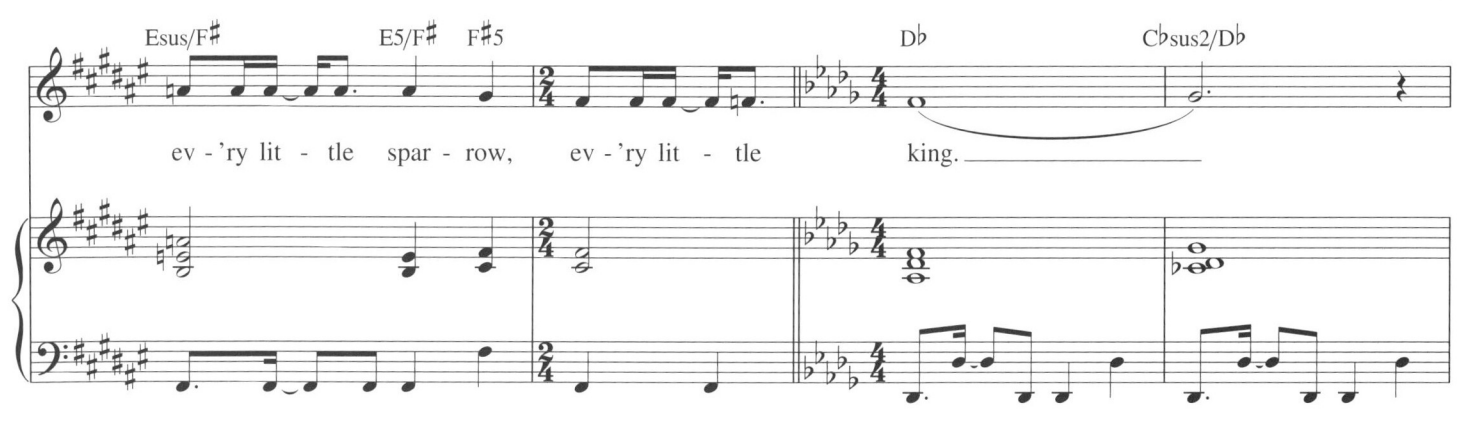
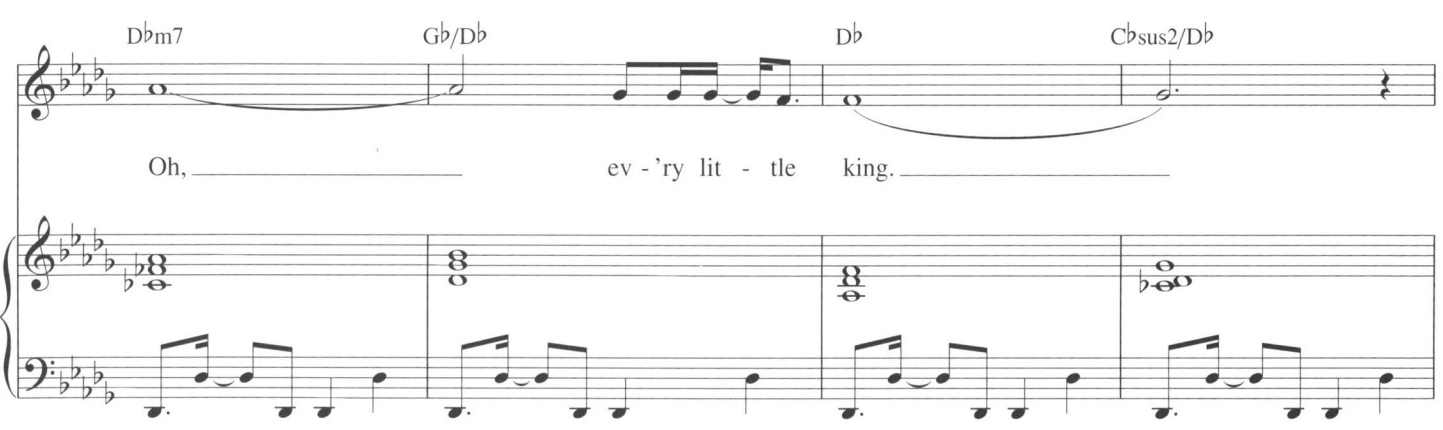
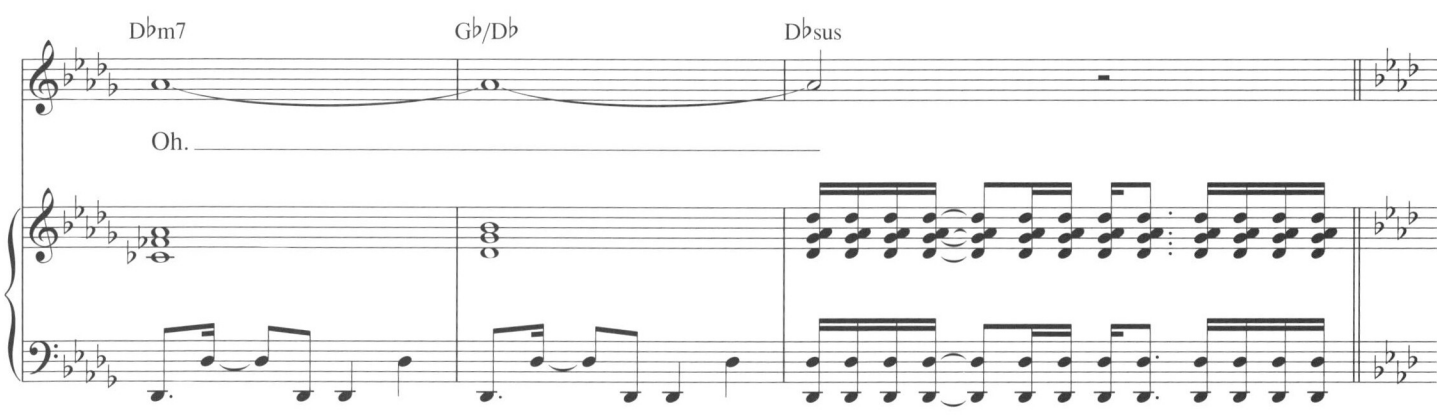

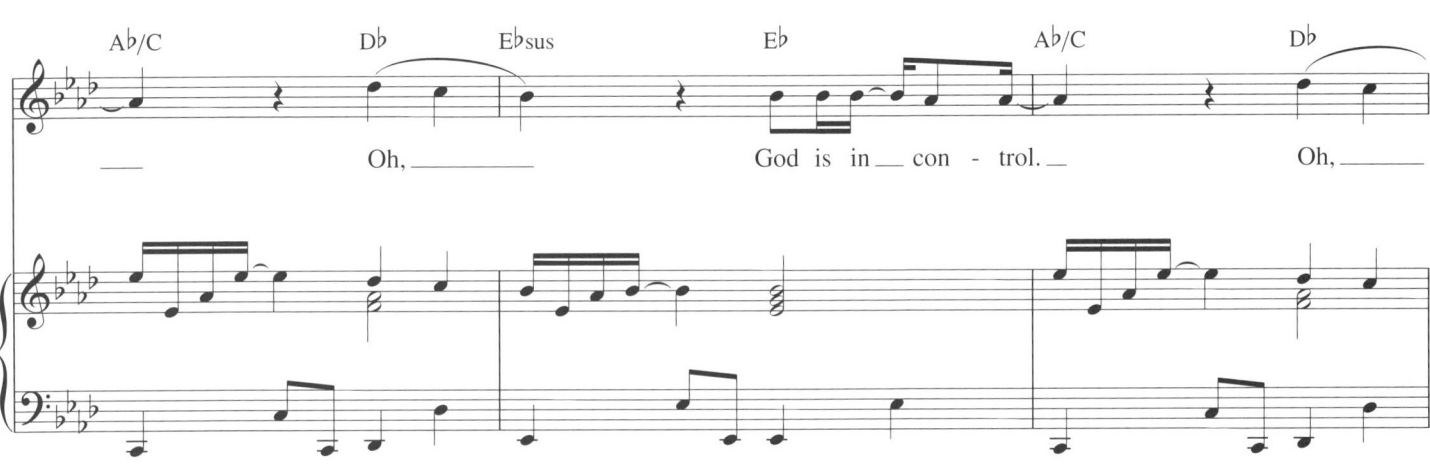
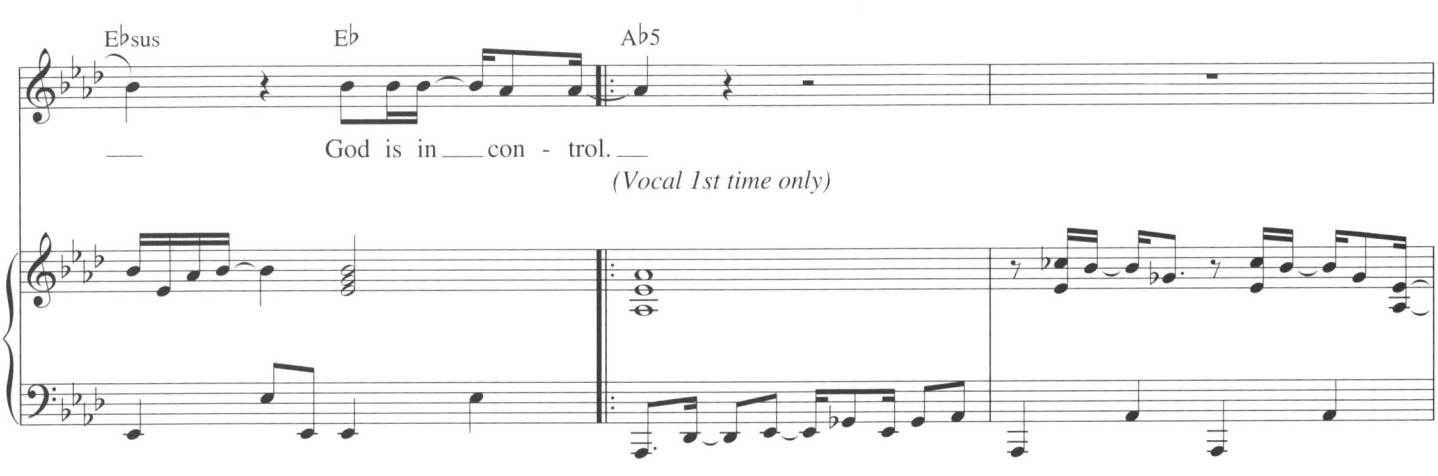

Healing Hands

Words and Music by GRANT CUNNINGHAM,
MATT HUESMANN and JONATHAN PIERCE

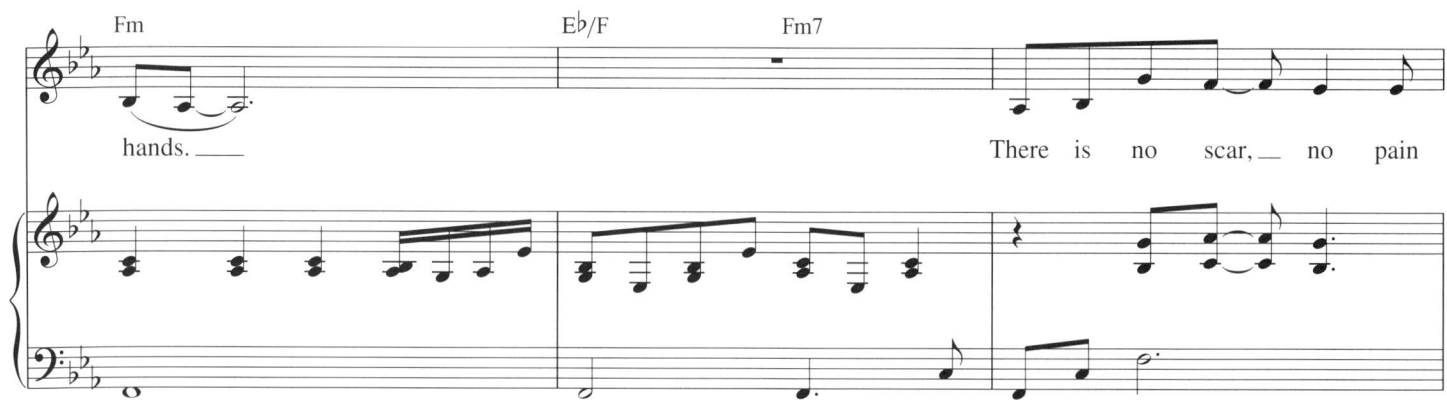
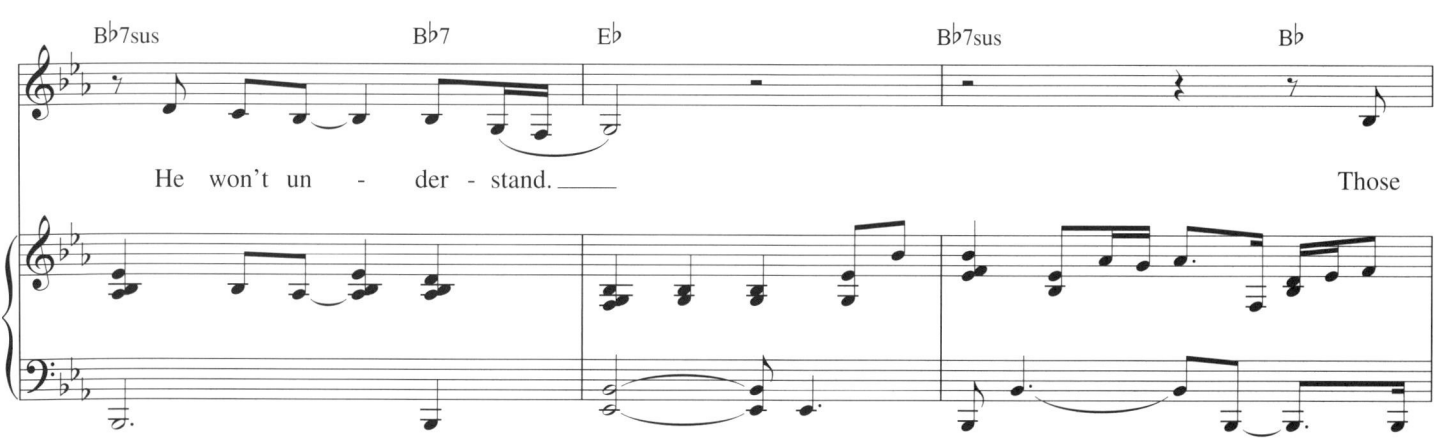

Copyright © 1994 by Careers-BMG Music Publishing, Inc., River Oaks Music and Curb Songs
All Rights for River Oaks Music Administered by EMI Christian Music Publishing
International Copyright Secured   All Rights Reserved

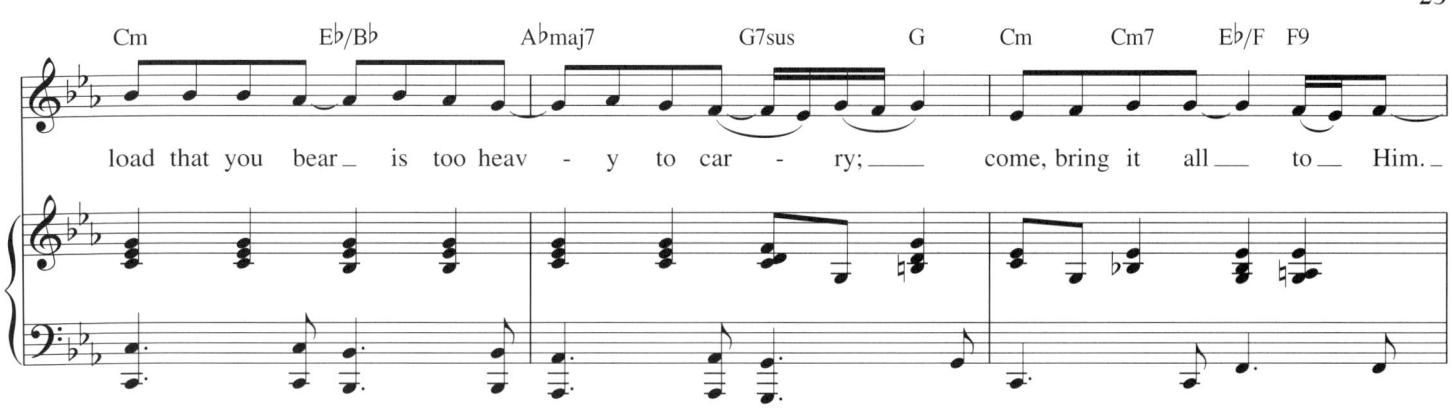

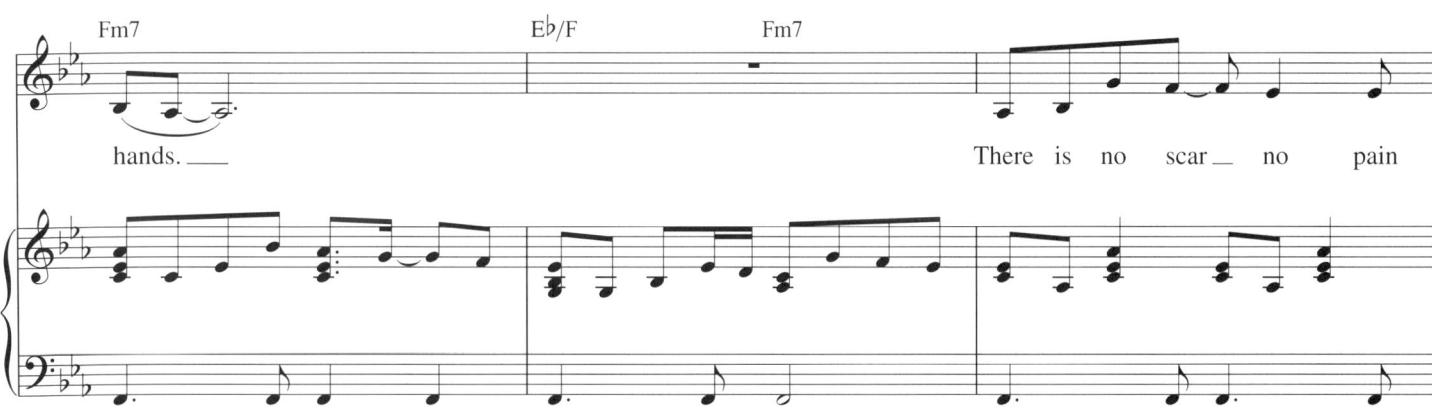
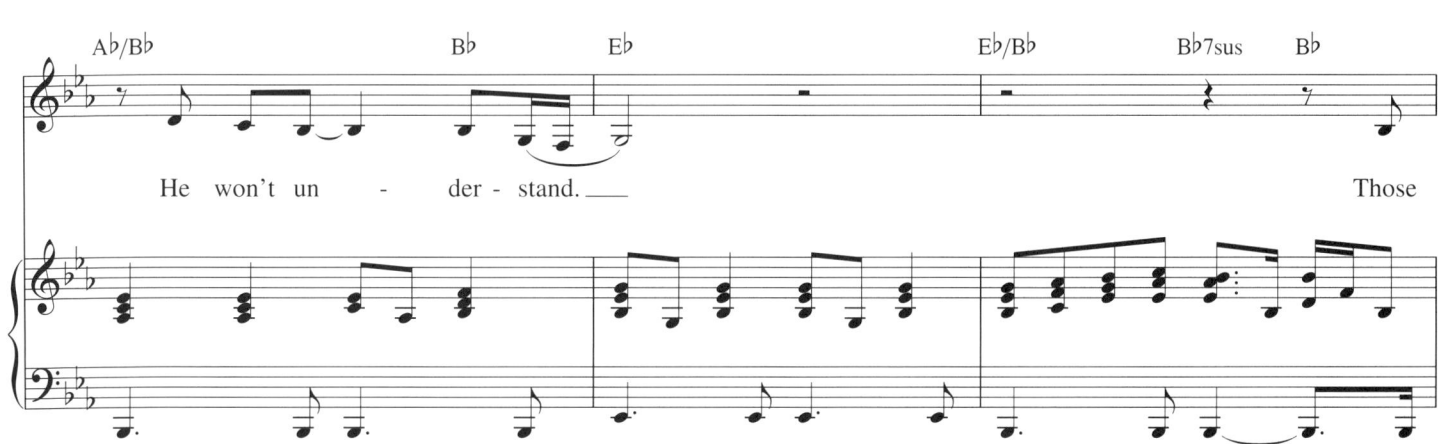

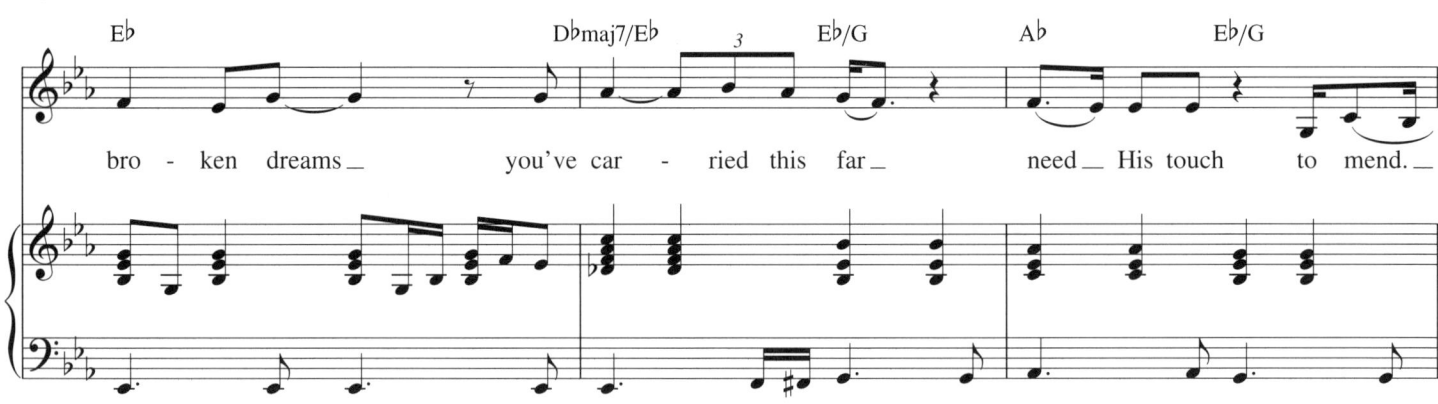

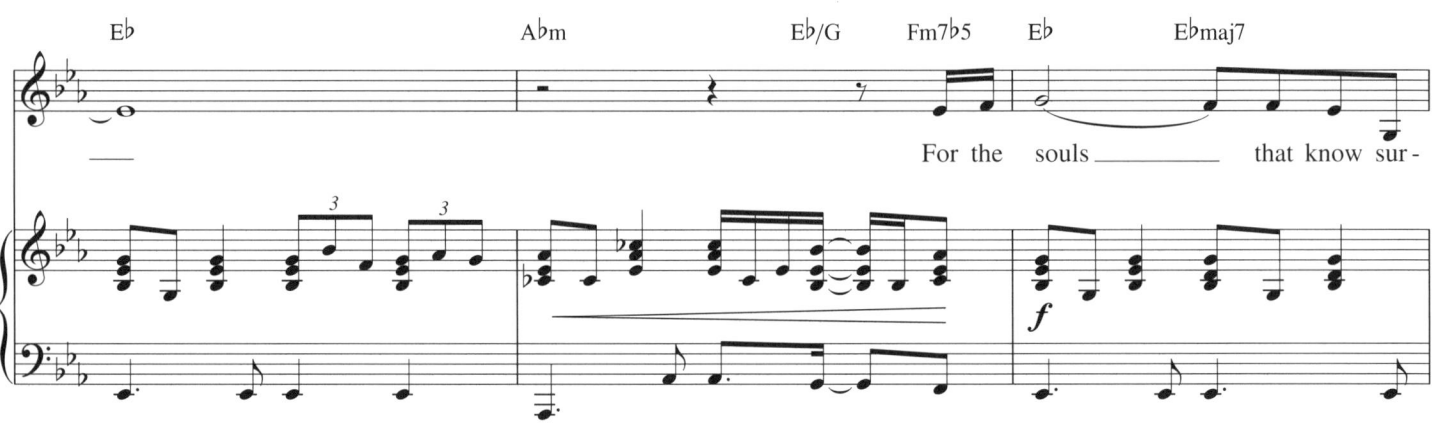

Heaven in the Real World

Words and Music by
STEVEN CURTIS CHAPMAN

© 1994 SPARROW SONG and PEACH HILL SONGS
Admin. by EMI CHRISTIAN MUSIC PUBLISHING
All Rights Reserved Used by Permission

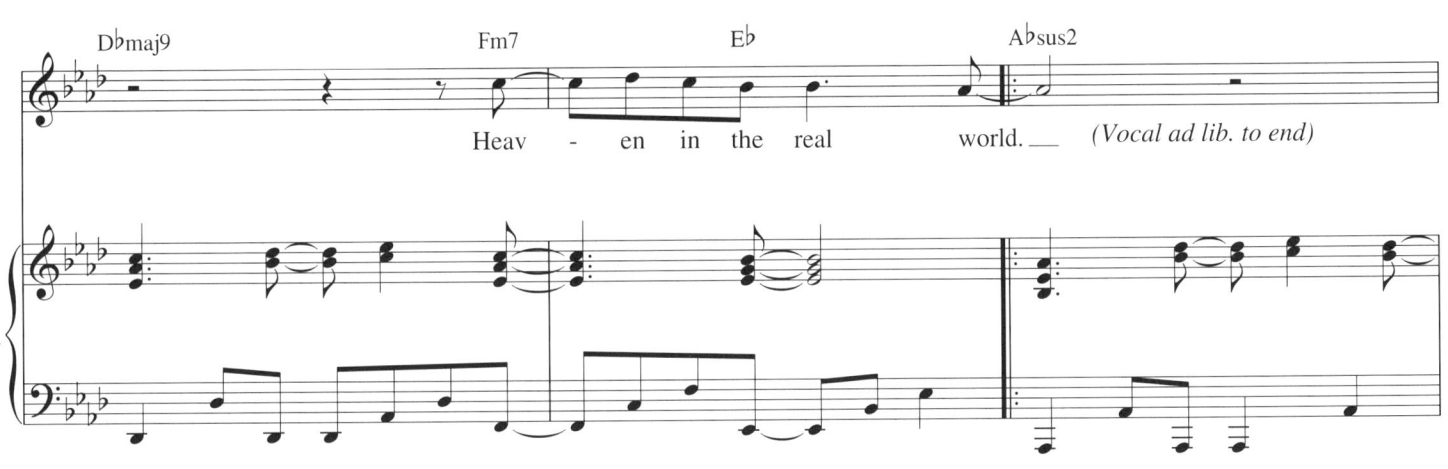

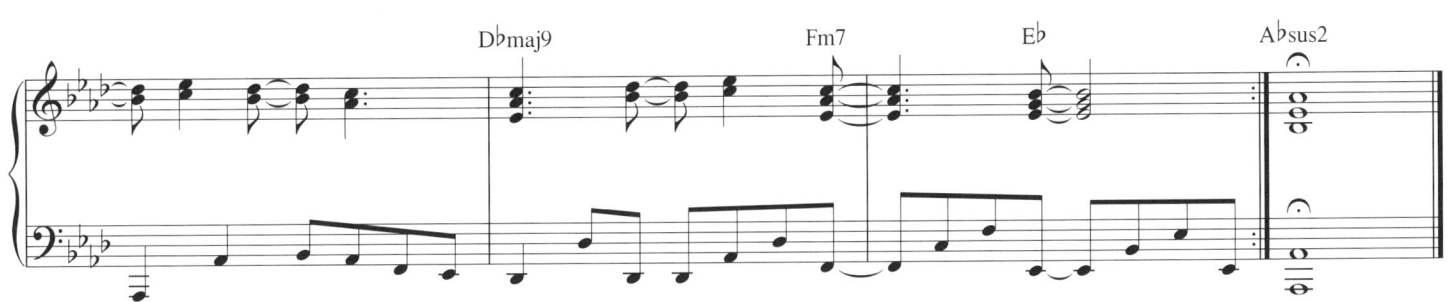

I Could Sing of Your Love Forever

Words and Music by
MARTIN SMITH

© 1994 CURIOUS? MUSIC (PRS)
Admin. in the U.S. and Canada by BIRDWING MUSIC, a d/b/a of EMI CHRISTIAN MUSIC PUBLISHING
All Rights Reserved Used by Permission

37

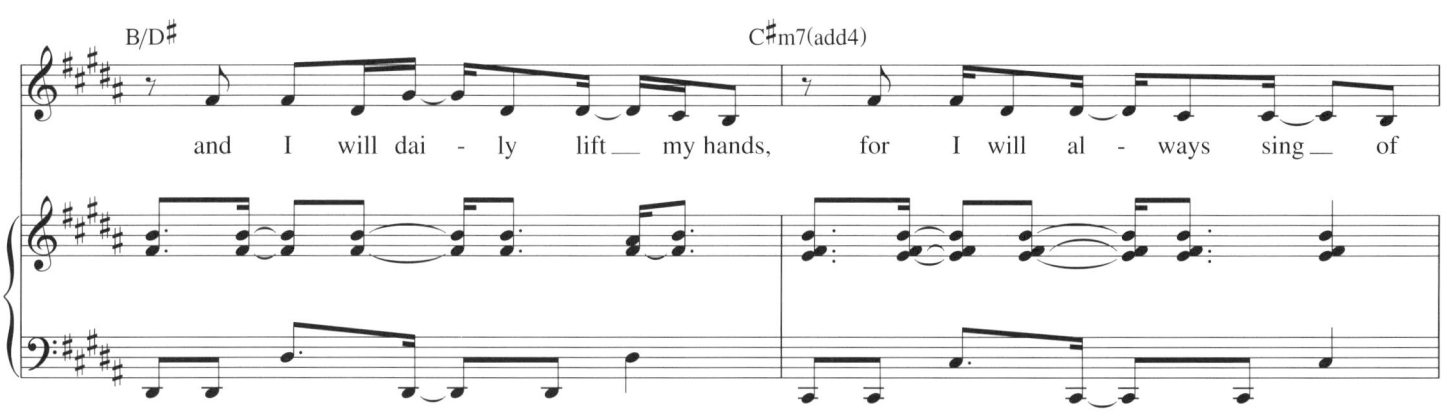

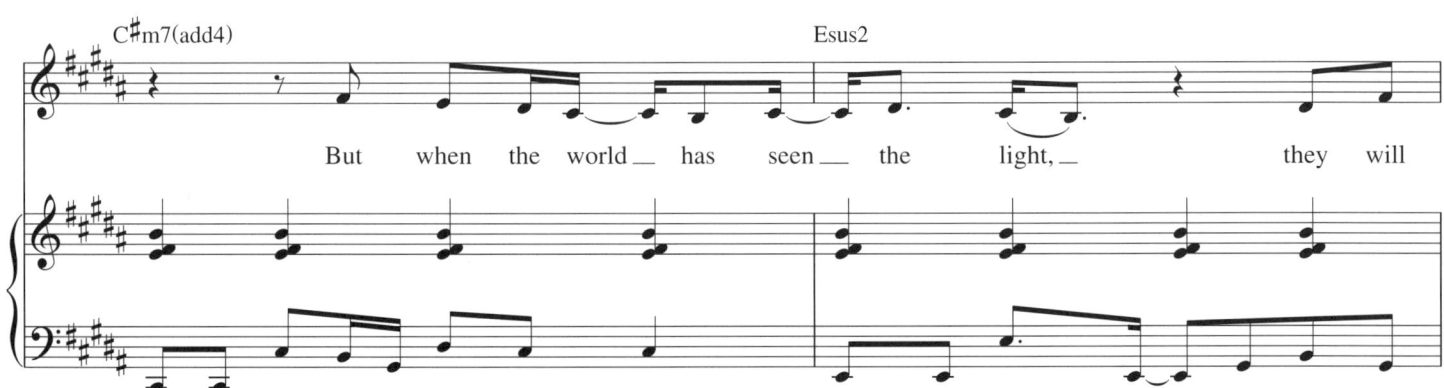

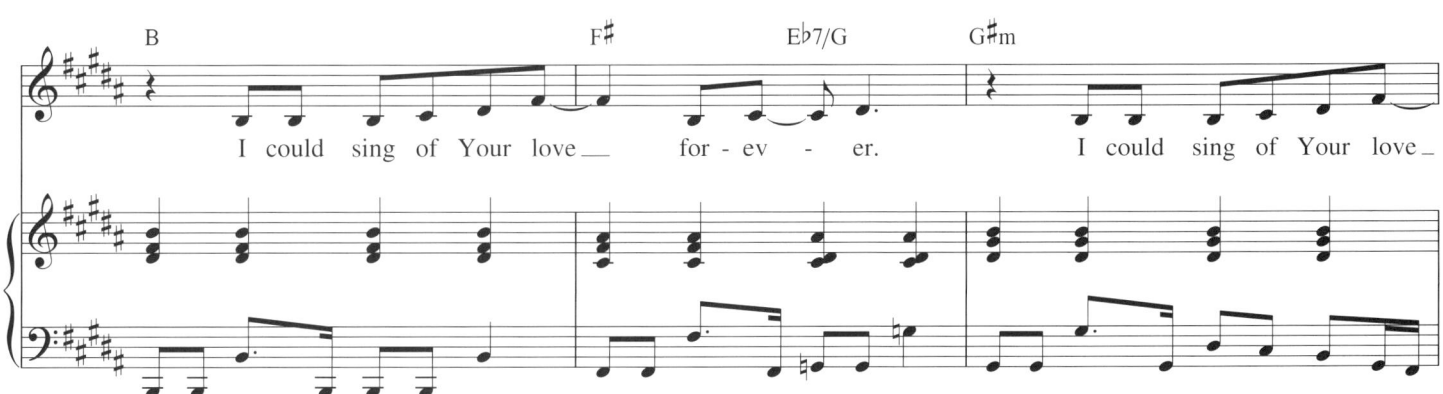

I Pledge Allegiance to the Lamb

Words and Music by
RAY BOLTZ

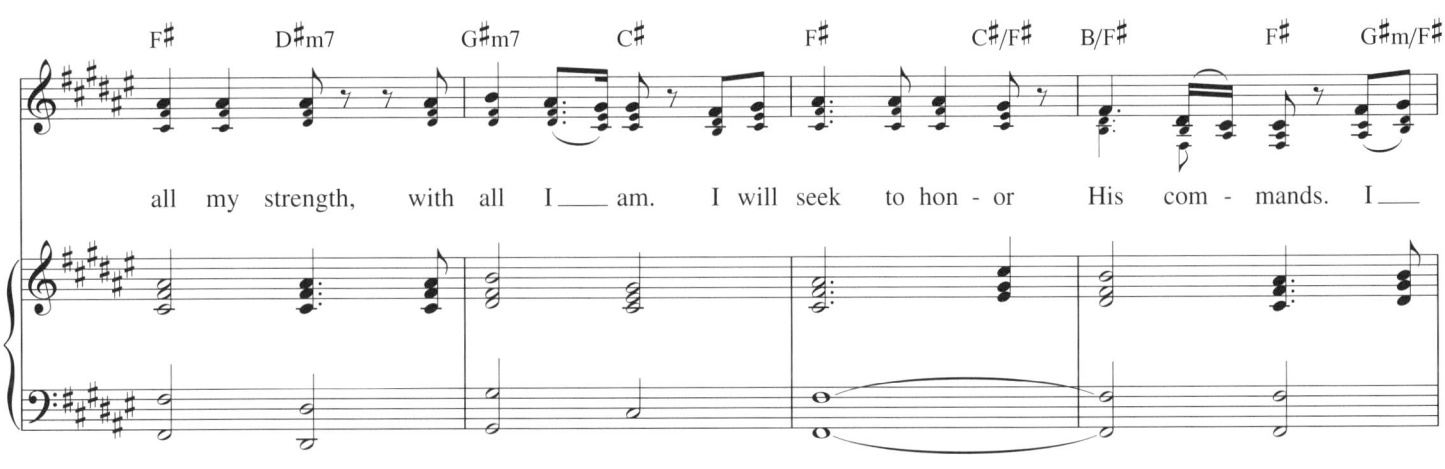

© 1994 Word Music, Inc. and Shepherd Boy Music (admin. by Word Music, Inc.)
All Rights Reserved Used by Permission

Let Us Pray

Words and Music by
STEVEN CURTIS CHAPMAN

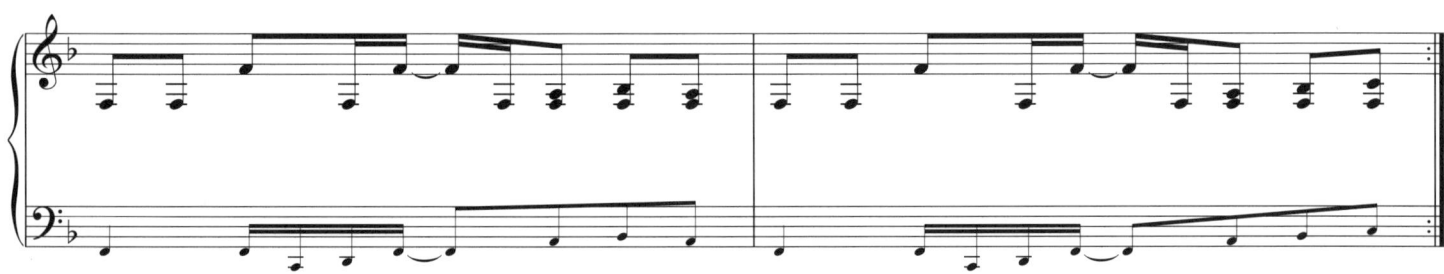
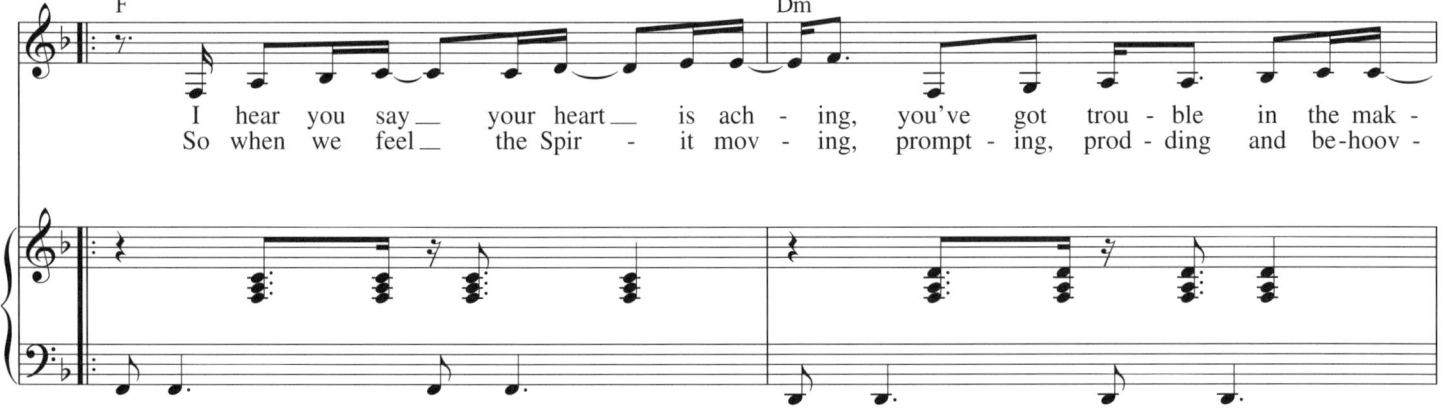

© 1996 SPARROW SONG and PEACH HILL SONGS
Admin. by EMI CHRISTIAN MUSIC PUBLISHING
All Rights Reserved   Used by Permission

A Place Called Grace

Words and Music by SHAWN CRAIG
and DAVE CLARK

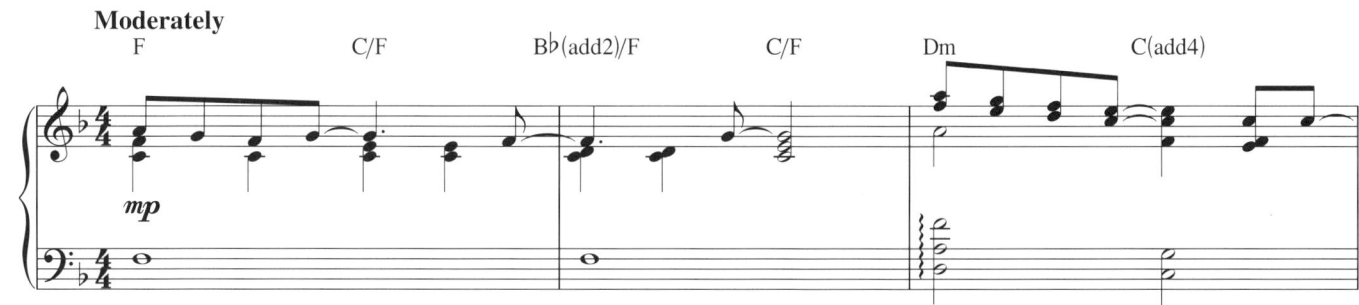

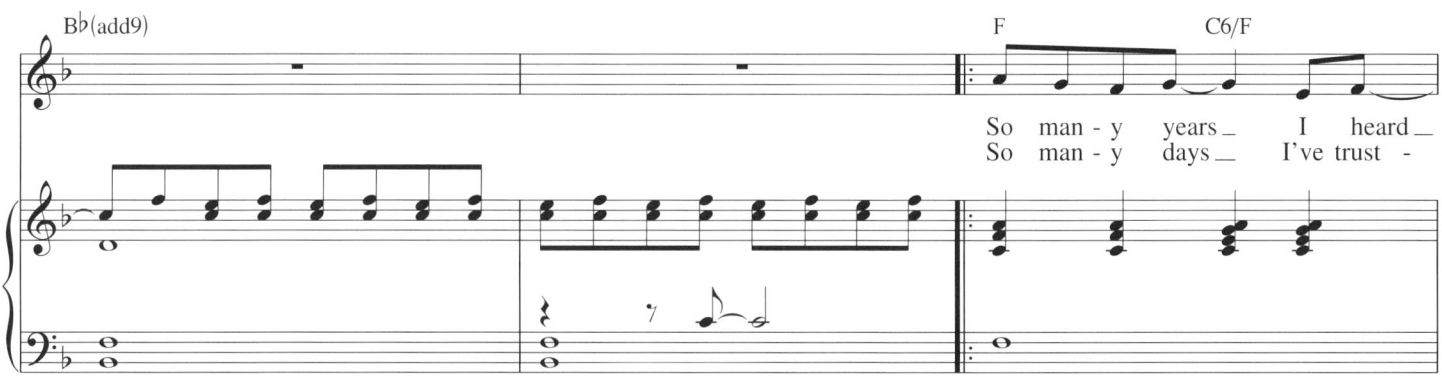

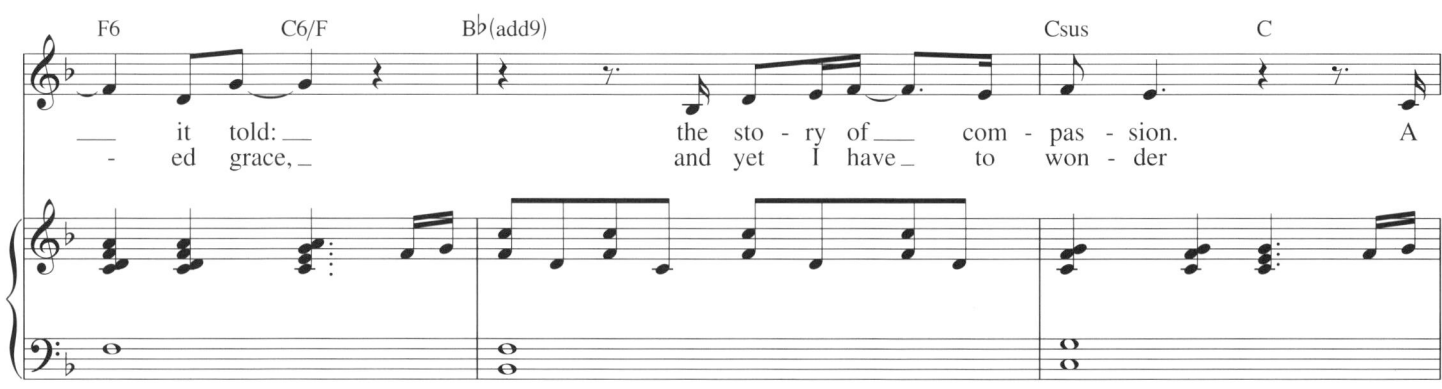

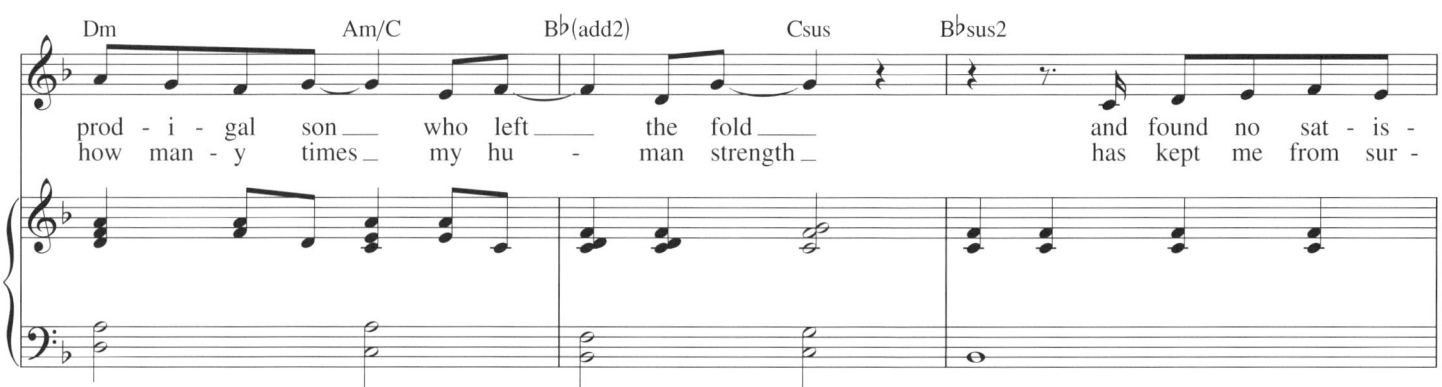

© 1999 ARIOSE MUSIC, PRAISE SONG PRESS, NEW SPRING PUBLISHING and CALLENDER LANE MUSIC
ARIOSE MUSIC and PRAISE SONG PRESS Admin. by EMI CHRISTIAN MUSIC PUBLISHING
NEW SPRING PUBLISHING and CALLENDER LANE MUSIC Admin. by BRENTWOOD-BENSON MUSIC PUBLISHING, INC.
All Rights Reserved   Used by Permission

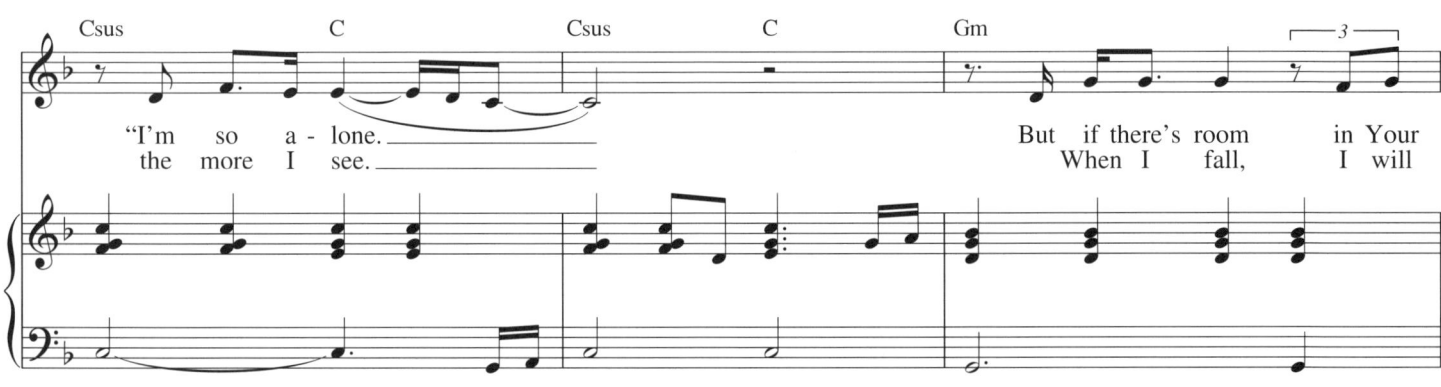

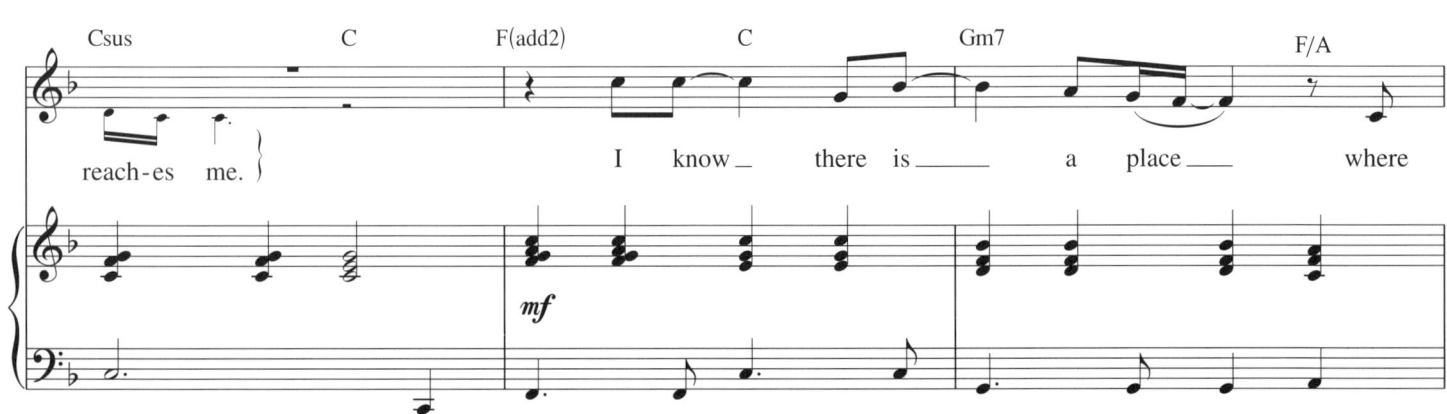

56

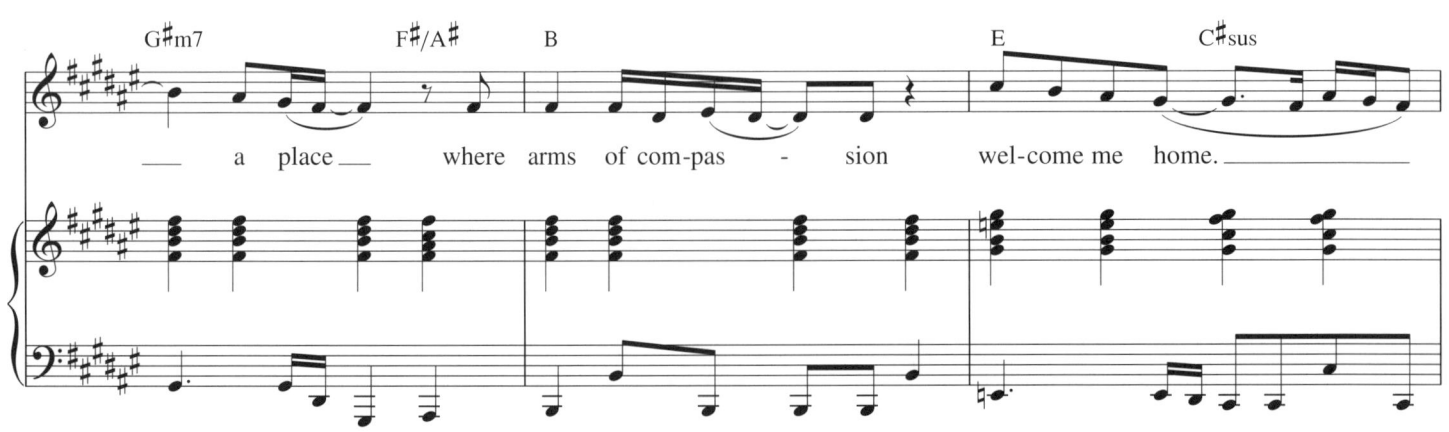

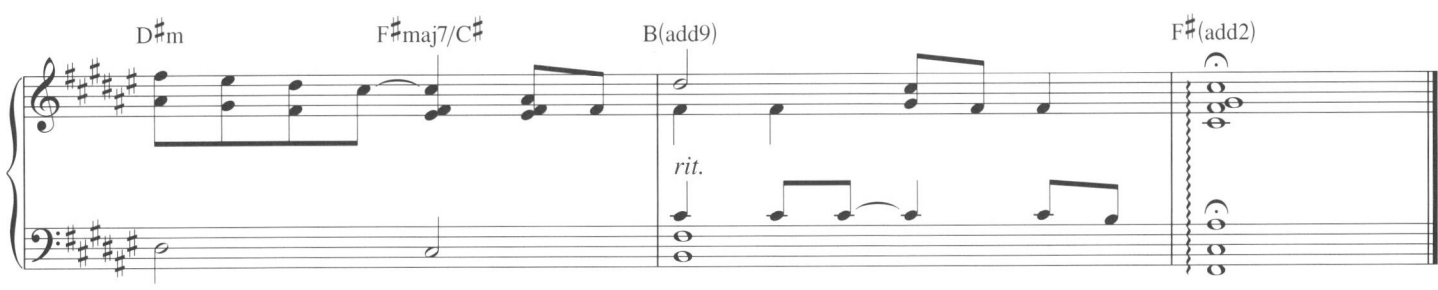

We Can Make a Difference

Words and Music by MARK HEIMERMANN
and DAVID MULLEN

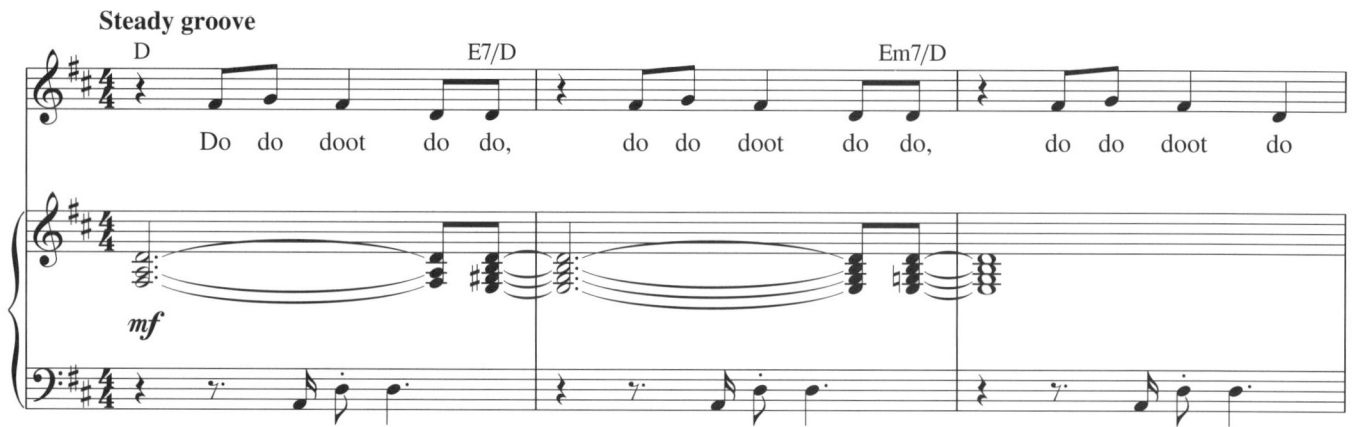

© 1996 Fun Attic Music, Word Music, Inc. and Seat Of The Pants Music (admin. by Word Music, Inc.)
All Rights Reserved   Used by Permission

60

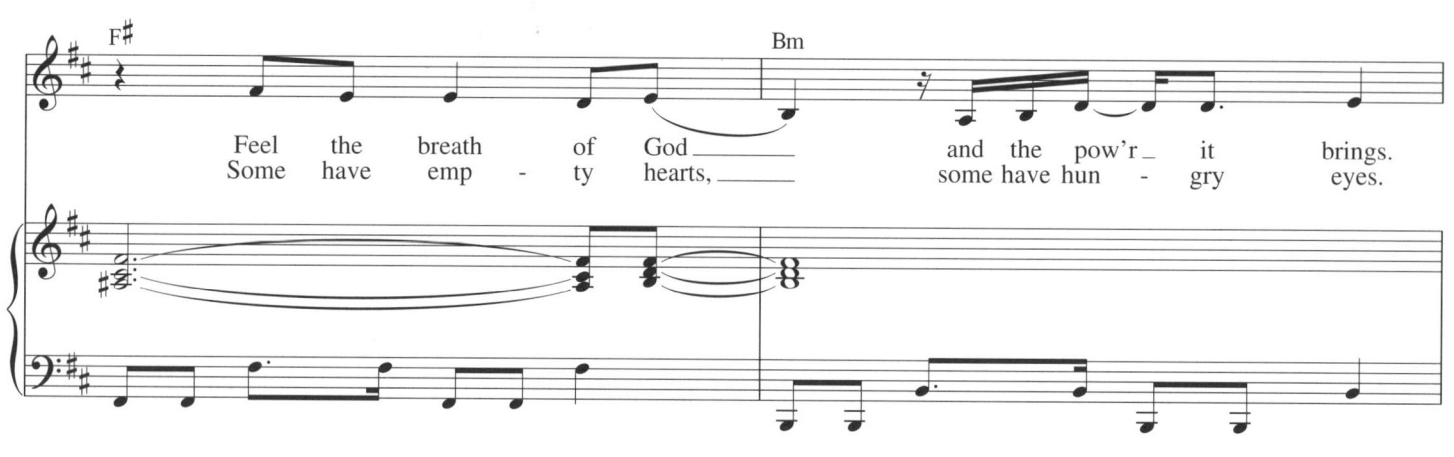

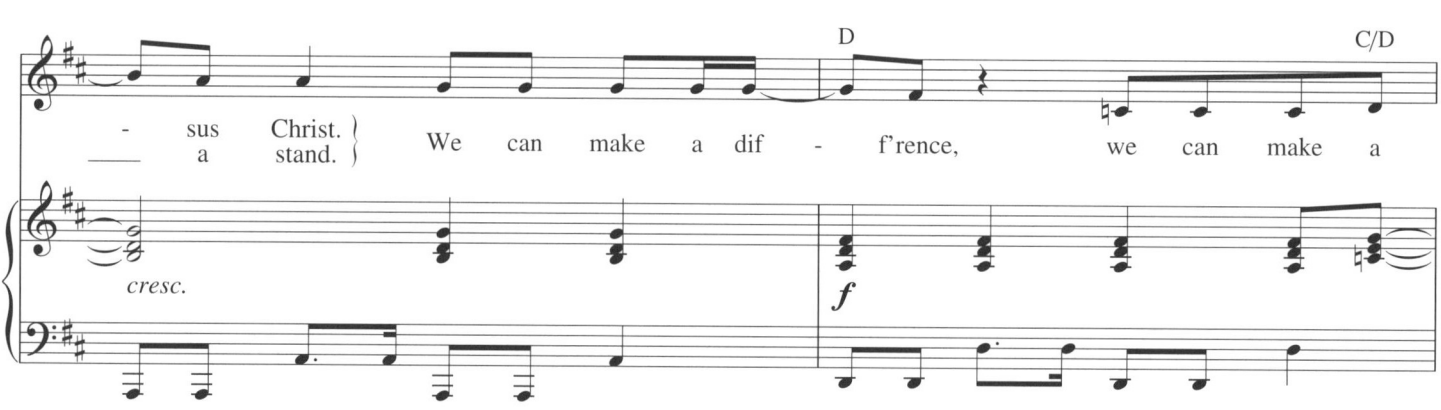

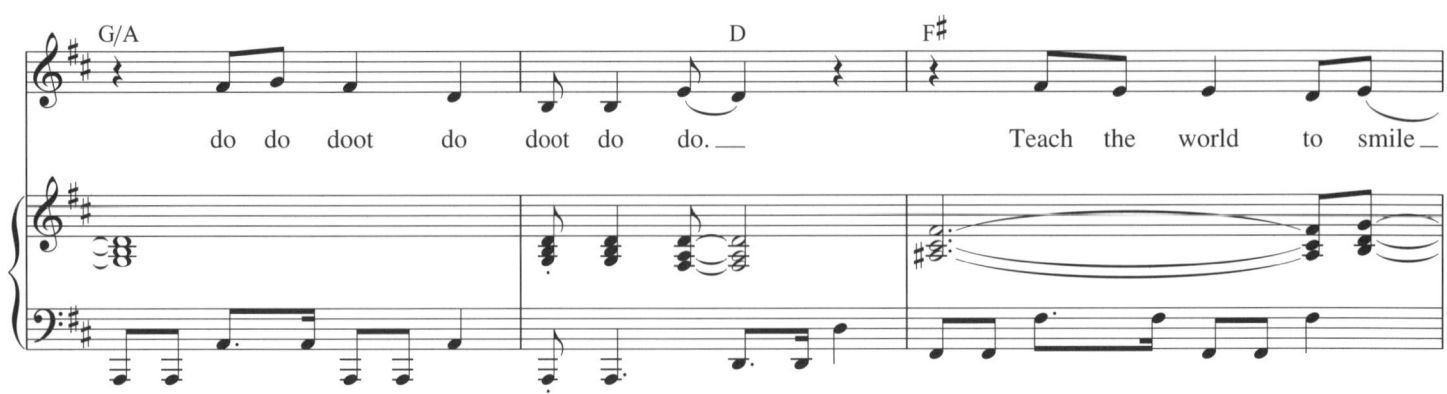
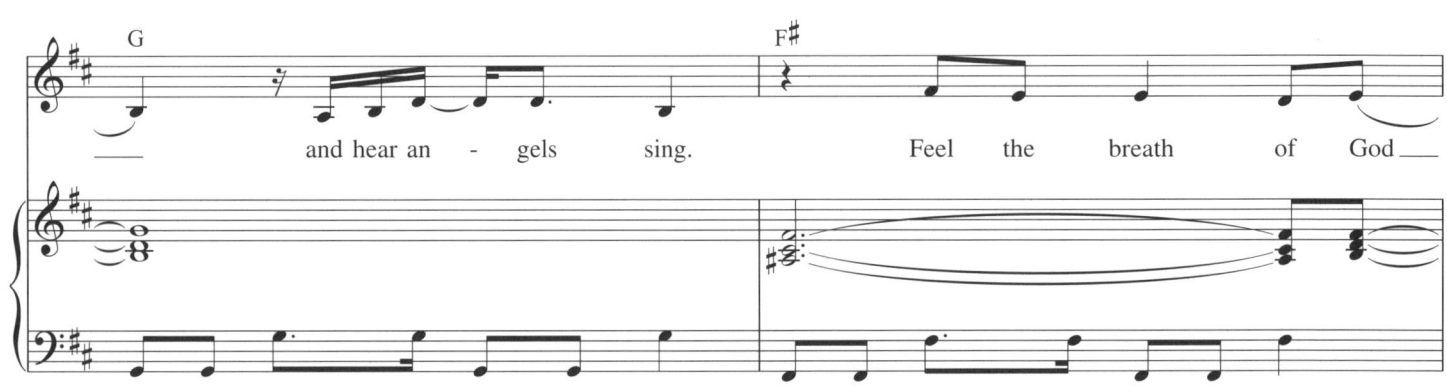
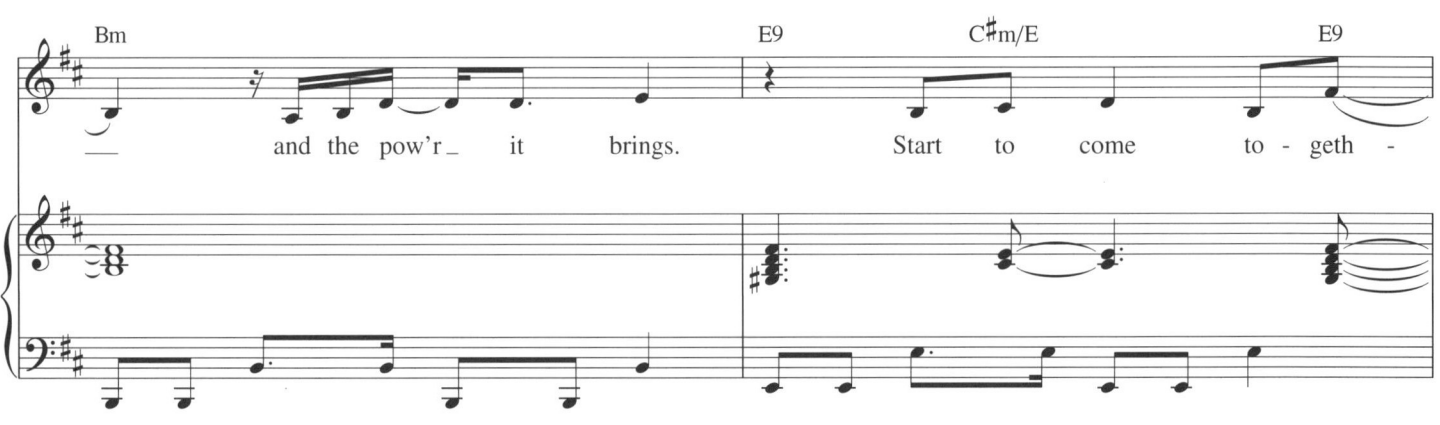

The Finest Inspirational Music
Songbooks arranged for piano, voice, and guitar.

40 SONGS FOR A BETTER WORLD
40 songs with a message, including: All You Need Is Love • Bless the Beasts and Children • Colors of the Wind • Everything Is Beautiful • He Ain't Heavy...He's My Brother • I Am Your Child • Love Can Build a Bridge • What a Wonderful World • What the World Needs Now Is Love • You've Got a Friend • more.
00310096..$15.95

BEST GOSPEL SONGS EVER
80 of the best-loved Gospel songs of all time, including: Amazing Grace • At Calvary • Because He Lives • Behold the Lamb • Daddy Sang Bass • Get All Excited • His Eye Is on the Sparrow • I Saw the Light • I'd Rather Have Jesus • I'll Fly Away • Just a Little Talk With Jesus • Mansion Over the Hilltop • My Tribute • Precious Lord, Take My Hand • and more.
00310503..$19.95

BUTTERFLY KISSES & OTHER CONTEMPORARY CHRISTIAN FAVORITES
This outstanding collection features the mega-hit title song and 19 more contempoorary Christian favorites: Children of the World • Crucified with Christ • Freedom • God Is in Control • Heaven in the Real World • Helping Hand • I Love the Lorrd • Jesus Will Still Be There • Say the Name • Signs of Life • Where You Belong • and more.
00310340..$12.95

CHRISTIAN CHILDREN'S SONGBOOK
Over 80 songs from Sunday School, including: Awesome God • The B-I-B-L-E • The Bible Tells Me So • Clap Your Hands • Day by Day • He's Got the Whole World in His Hands • I Am a C-H-R-I-S-T-I-A-N • I'm in the Lord's Army • If You're Happy (And You Know It) • Jesus Loves Me • Kum Ba Yah • Let There Be Peace on Earth • This Little Light of Mine • When the Saints Go Marching In • and more.
00310472..$19.95

For More Information, See Your Local Music Dealer, Or Write To:

HAL•LEONARD® CORPORATION
7777 W. Bluemound Rd. P.O. Box 13819 Milwaukee, WI 53213

Visit us at www.halleonard.com for a complete listing of titles.

Prices, contents, and availability subject to change without notice. Some products may not be available outside the U.S.A.

CHRISTIAN WEDDING SONGBOOK
Over 30 contemporary Christian wedding favorites, including: Bonded Together • Butterfly Kisses • Commitment Song • Flesh of My Flesh • Go There with You • Household of Faith • How Beautiful • Love Will Be Our Home • Make Us One • Parent's Prayer (Let Go of Two) • This Is the Day (A Wedding Song) • and more.
00310681..$16.95

CONTEMPORARY CHRISTIAN VOCAL GROUP FAVORITES
15 songs, including: The Basics of Life • A Few Good Men • The Great Divide • Undivided • and more.

00310019..$10.95

CONTEMPORARY CHRISTIAN WEDDING SONGBOOK
30 appropriate songs for weddings, including: Household of Faith • Love in Any Language • Love Will Be Our Home • Parents' Prayer • This Is Love • Where There Is Love • and more.
00310022..$14.95

COUNTRY/GOSPEL U.S.A.
50 songs written for piano/guitar/four-part vocal. Highlights: An American Trilogy • Daddy Sang Bass • He Set Me Free • I Saw the Light • I'll Meet You in the Morning • Kum Ba Yah • Mansion Over the Hilltop • Love Lifted Me • Turn Your Radio On • When the Saints Go Marching In • many more.
00240139..$10.95

ETERNAL GLORY
42 songs of comfort and hope, including: Amazing Grace • Ave Maria (Schubert) • Because He Lives • Deep River • For All the Saints • Friends • His Eye Is on the Sparrow • Home Free • How Great Thou Art • If You Could See Me Now • It Is Well with My Soul • Just a Closer Walk with Thee • Panis Angelicus (O Lord Most Holy) • Peace in the Valley • Rock of Ages • When We All Get to Heaven • You'll Never Walk Alone • and more.
00310742..$12.95

GREAT HYMNS TREASURY
A comprehensive collection of 70 favorites: Close to Thee • Footsteps of Jesus • Amazing Grace • At the Cross • Blessed Assurance • Blest Be the Tie That Binds • Church in the Wildwood • The Church's One Foundation • His Eye Is on the Sparrow • How Firm a Foundation • I Love to Tell the Story • In the Garden • The Old Rugged Cross • We're Marching to Zion • Were You There? • What a Friend We Have in Jesus • When I Survey The Wondrous Cross • more.
00310167..$12.95

OUR GOD REIGNS
A collection of over 70 songs of praise and worship, including: El Shaddai • Find Us Faithful • His Eyes • Holy Ground • How Majestic Is Your Name • Proclaim the Glory of the Lord • Sing Your Praise to the Lord • Thy Word • and more.
00311695......................$17.95

THE PRAYER OF JABEZ
7 original songs inspired by the book *The Prayer of Jabez*. Titles include: This Is My Prayer (Sarah Sadler/Margaret Becker) • The Prayer of Jabez (Geoff Moore/Steve Reischl) • Be in Your Blessing (Erin O'Donnell/Adrienne Liesching) • Beyond the Borders (Jamie Rowe/Steve Reischl) • Touch of Greatness (Geoff Moore/Phil Keaggy) • Lead Me Away (Rebecca St. James/Michael Tait) • The Day Is Dawning (Jill Phillips/Kevin Max).
00306458..$12.95

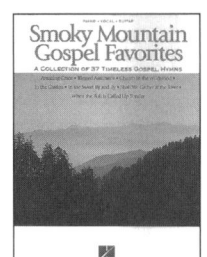

SMOKY MOUNTAIN GOSPEL FAVORITES
37 favorites, including: Amazing Grace • Blessed Assurance • Church in the Wildwood • I Love to Tell the Story • In the Garden • In the Sweet By and By • The Old Rugged Cross • Rock of Ages • Shall We Gather at the River • Wayfaring Stranger • What a Friend We Have in Jesus • When the Roll Is Called Up Yonder • When We All Get to Heaven • and more.
00310161..$8.95

ULTIMATE GOSPEL – 100 SONGS OF DEVOTION
Includes: El Shaddai • His Eye Is on the Sparrow • How Great Thou Art • Just a Closer Walk with Thee • Lead Me, Guide Me • (There'll Be) Peace in the Valley (For Me) • Precious Lord, Take My Hand • Wings of a Dove • more.
00241009..$19.95